A gift for:

From:

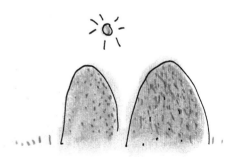

Other books in this series:

The Secrets of Happiness 365   Yes to life! 365   Inspiration 365

Words to live by 365   Friendship 365   For my Daughter 365

Illustrated by Joanna Kidney
Edited by Helen Exley

Published in 2014 and 2021 by Helen Exley®LONDON in Great Britain.

The moral right of the author has been asserted. Acknowledgements: The publishers are grateful
for permission to reproduce copyright material. Whilst every reasonable effort has been made to trace copyright holders,
the publishers would be pleased to hear from any not here acknowledged. Words by Pam Brown, Mark Burnett,
Jenny de Vries, Daniel Dilling, Tracey Dowson, Pamela Dugdale, Helen Exley, Susan Squellati Florence, Clive Garland,
Mandy Gibson, Zaryk Glasson, Charlotte Gray, M. Gurr, Allison Huddart, Adrian Knight, Stuart and Linda MacFarlane,
Morwenna Pond, Meghan Simmons, Emma Smith, Lisa Stanley, Helen Thomson, Andrew Trowbridge, Lee Walker,
Kevin Williams © Helen Exley Creative Ltd 2014, 2021. The illustrations by Joanna Kidney © Joanna Kidney 2014, 2021.
Design, selection and arrangement © Helen Exley Creative Ltd 2014, 2021.

ISBN 978-1-84634-561-6   12   11   10   9

MIX
Paper from
responsible sources
FSC® C081635

Helen Exley®LONDON, 16 Chalk Hill, Watford, Hertfordshire, WD19 4BG, UK
www.helenexley.com

Nothing is worth
more than this day.

JOHANN WOLFGANG VON GOETHE
(1749 – 1832)

If you love this book...

...you can find
other HELEN EXLEY® books like it on
www.helenexley.com

Helen Exley and her team have specialised in finding wonderful
quotations for gifts of happiness, wisdom, calm and between families,
friends and loved ones... A major part of Helen's work is to bring
love and communication within families by finding and publishing the
things people everywhere would like to say to the people they love.

Her books obviously strike a chord because they now appear in forty-five
languages, and are distributed in more than eighty countries.

You can follow us on ◼f and ◉

There's joy all around us!
Why wait till tomorrow?
We've only this moment to
live. A heaven within us
is ours for the finding.
A freedom no riches can give!

J. DONALD WALTERS

This is the best day the world has ever seen.
Tomorrow will be better.

R. A. CAMPBELL

Laughter is the joyous
universal evergreen of life.

ABRAHAM LINCOLN
(1809 – 1865)

The sun rises on a new day
scattering yesterday into memories.
No matter what troubled you
in the past, the future is full
of opportunities, full of hope.

STUART & LINDA MACFARLANE

Happiness is a wonderful
feeling. It makes you feel
good in any situation.
It gives you hope in times
of despair. It makes you feel
peace in a world of turmoil.

BILLY MILLS (DAKOTA)
WITH NICHOLAS SPARKS

December 29

There is beauty around us, in things
large and small, in friends, family,
the countryside, a singing bird.
Stop to reflect, to give thanks,
to contemplate the gift of another day.
Touch the wonders of life and rejoice.

ANTON CHEKHOV (1860 – 1904)

That it will never come again is what makes life so sweet.

EMILY DICKINSON
(1830 – 1886)

December 28

If I were to choose the sights, the sounds, the fragrances
I most would want... on a final day on earth, I think I would
choose these: the clear, ethereal song of a white-throated sparrow
singing at dawn; the smell of pine trees in the heat of noon;
the lonely calling of Canada geese; the sight of a dragon-fly
glinting in the sunshine...

EDWIN WAY TEALE (1899 – 1980)

If you want to be happy, be.

LEO TOLSTOY (1828 – 1910)

December 27

When we really love and accept
and approve of ourselves exactly as we are,
then everything in life works. It's as if little
miracles are everywhere.

LOUISE L. HAY, B.1926

Wake up with a smile – make
this the best day of your life.

STUART & LINDA MACFARLANE

December 26

I'm filled with joy
when the day dawns quietly
over the roof of the sky.

ESKIMO SONG

A cheery smile
each joy will double,
And cut in half
your every trouble.

AUTHOR UNKNOWN

The happiness of life is made
up of minute fractions – the little,
soon-forgotten charities of a kiss,
a smile, a kind look,
a heartfelt compliment.

SAMUEL TAYLOR COLERIDGE
(1772 – 1834)

The earth laughs in flowers.

RALPH WALDO EMERSON (1803-1882)

Winter is on my head,
but eternal spring is in
my heart.

VICTOR HUGO (1802 – 1885)

Live in the present,
do all the things
that need to be done.
Do all the good
you can each day.
The future will unfold.

PEACE PILGRIM

Joys are our wings.

JEAN PAUL RICHTER (1763 – 1825)

Joy is not in things;
it is in us.

RICHARD WAGNER
(1813 – 1883)

Let yourself be silently drawn by the strange pull of what you really love. It will not lead you astray.

JALAL AL-DIN RUMI (1207 – 1273)

Today is your day – the day
when you can change your life.

STUART & LINDA MACFARLANE

When the day returns, call us up with morning faces and with morning hearts, eager to labour, happy if happiness be our portion, and if the day be marked for sorrow, strong to endure.

ROBERT LOUIS STEVENSON (1850 – 1894)

Keep knocking
and the joy inside will eventually
open a window
and look out to see who is there.

JALAL AL-DIN RUMI
(1207 – 1273)

In the depth of winter, I finally learned that within me there lay an invincible summer.

ALBERT CAMUS (1913 – 1960)

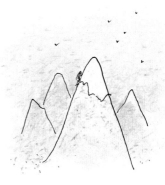

Happiness is the whole world as friends.
It's light all through your life.

DANIEL DILLING, AGE 8

Happiness is the art
of making a bouquet of those
flowers within reach.

BOB GODDARD

For new, and new,
and ever-new,
The golden bud within the blue;
And every morning
seems to say:
"There's something happy
on the way..."

HENRY VAN DYKE (1852 – 1933)

To watch the corn grow, and the blossoms set;
to draw hard breath over ploughshare or spade;
to read, to think, to love, to hope, to pray, – these
are the things that make people happy.

JOHN RUSKIN (1819 – 1900)

Life is fun
Life is happiness
Life is gladness
Life is loving
Life is helping
Life is gentleness
Life is laughter
Oh, life is beautiful.

ALLISON HUDDART, AGE 10

Today, today, today.
Bless us… and help
us to grow.

ROSH HASHANAH LITURGY

Wear a smile.
One size fits all.

AUTHOR UNKNOWN

Happiness is not
a station you
arrive at, but a
manner of traveling.

MARGARET LEE RUNBECK

I am grateful for what I am and have.
My thanksgiving is perpetual. It is surprising how
contented one can be with nothing definite –
only a sense of existence…

HENRY DAVID THOREAU (1817 – 1862)

May this be one of the days…

…when the mind discovers undreamed-of things.

…when the eye is overwhelmed by glory.

…may this be one of the days of new beginning when

we seem to see to the very edges of the universe.

PAM BROWN

Happiness
is a gift we can all
afford to give.

PAM BROWN

There is no cure
for birth and death,
save to enjoy the interval.

GEORGE SANTAYANA (1863 – 1952)

Enjoy life, employ life.
It flits away and will not stay.

PROVERB

To be happy, drop the words "if only" and substitute instead the words "next time."

DR. SMILEY BLANTON (1882 – 1966)

Let us be grateful to people
who make us happy;
they are the charming gardeners
who make us blossom.

MARCEL PROUST (1871 – 1922)

Smiling is infectious.

BILL CULLEN, B.1942

I am beginning to learn that it is the sweet, simple things of life which are the real ones after all.

LAURA INGALLS WILDER (1867 – 1957)

There are dark days in every life,
but it is very rare that we cannot find
some small delight to give us hope,
a glimmer of light that penetrates
the cloud and reminds us of the
hidden radiance.

PAM BROWN

When a person
is too tired to give you a smile,
give them one of yours.

AUTHOR UNKNOWN

The rarest feeling that ever
lights a human face is the contentment
of a loving soul.

HENRY WARD BEECHER (1813 – 1887)

To be able to find joy
in another's joy:
that is the secret of
happiness.

GEORGES BERNANOS
(1888 – 1948)

Happiness is when
what you think, what you say,
and what you do,
are in harmony.

MAHATMA GANDHI (1869 – 1948)

The sun does not shine
for a few trees and flowers,
but for the wide world's joy.

HENRY WARD BEECHER (1813 – 1887)

May the future bring
every happiness, the fulfilment
of your dreams, many friends
and lasting love.

PAM BROWN

...happiness comes through doors and windows we did not even know we opened.

FROM "THE FRIENDSHIP BOOK OF FRANCIS GAY"

People don't notice whether it's winter
or summer when they're happy.

ANTON CHEKHOV (1860 – 1904)

Happiness is an inside job.

H. JACKSON BROWN SENIOR

Think of all
the beauty that's still
left in and around you
and be happy!

ANNE FRANK (1929 – 1945)

January 28

The sun and stars that float
in the open air…
the apple-shaped Earth
and we upon it…
surely the drift of
them is something grand;
I do not know what it is
except that it is grand,
and that it is happiness…

WALT WHITMAN (1819 – 1892)

A happy life is not built up of tours abroad
and pleasant holidays, but of little clumps of violets
noticed by the roadside.

DR. EDWARD A. WILSON

Everyone must have felt that a cheerful friend is like a sunny day, which sheds its brightness on all around; and most of us can, as we choose, make of this world either a palace or a prison.

SIR JOHN LUBBOCK (1834 – 1913)

May you find happiness
and hold it safe.

PAM BROWN

May you sleep sound
and wake to sunlight.

PAM BROWN

There is not one day
of your life that is worth
wasting being sad.
Be Happy!!

STUART & LINDA MACFARLANE

How good is life, the mere living!
How fit to employ all the heart and the soul
and the senses forever in joy!

ROBERT BROWNING (1812 – 1889)

Enjoy the blessings of the day...
and the evils bear patiently; for this day only is ours:
we are dead to yesterday, and not born to tomorrow.

JEREMY TAYLOR (1613 – 1667)

Cheerful people are like
sunshine, cheering up
everybody around them...

HENRY WARD BEECHER
(1813 – 1887)

In the woods I am blessed.
Happy is everyone in the woods.
What glory in the woodland.

LUDWIG VAN BEETHOVEN
(1770 – 1827)

Do not linger to gather flowers to keep them,
but walk on, for flowers will keep themselves
blooming all your way.

RABINDRANATH TAGORE (1861 – 1941)

Every day, in every way,
I'm getting better and better.

ÉMILE COUÉ (1857 – 1926)

Keep love in your heart.
A life without it is like a sunless garden
when the flowers are dead.
The consciousness of loving and being loved
brings a warmth and richness to life
that nothing else can bring.

OSCAR WILDE (1854 – 1900)

May you wake to sunlight,
stretch out your arms to
embrace the day.

CHARLOTTE GRAY

...happiness is not simply
a destination,
it is a method of traveling
the road of life.

ELLEN R. WEINER

J oy is an ocean – we can scoop it up by the bucketful and there will always be plenty more.

STUART & LINDA MACFARLANE

So many reasons
to be happy...
Family
Friends
Freedom
Love
Music
Sport
Laughter
You are ALIVE!

STUART & LINDA MACFARLANE

On a most ordinary day
something wonderful can happen.
Out of the commonplace may come
the sight of something remarkable.
Music that overturns the heart.
A sentence that illuminates the mind.
An astonishment. A friend.
These are no ordinary days.

PAM BROWN

Each day the first day:
Each day a life.

DAG HAMMARSKJÖLD
(1905 – 1961)

A little health,
a little wealth, a little house
and freedom. And at the end,
a little friend, and little cause
to need him.

FROM AN OLD
ENGLISH SAMPLER

To have lived long enough to see the sun,
the dapple of leaves, star-studded skies
and kindly faces – to have heard the wind,
birdsong, loving voices, to have touched
a little cat, a woollen blanket, a flower,
to have tasted clear water, fresh bread, honey,
to have breathed the perfume of a rose
– is enough to make any life worth the living.

PAM BROWN

It ain't no use to grumble
and complain;
It's jest as cheap and easy
to rejoice...

JAMES WHITCOMB RILEY (1849 – 1916)

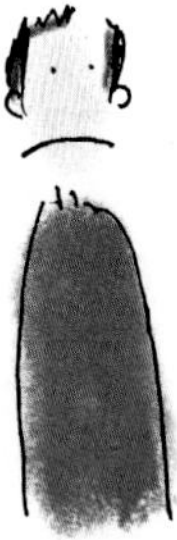

I do not fear tomorrow,
for I have seen yesterday –
and I love today.

WILLIAM ALLEN WHITE

Ten thousand flowers in spring, the moon in autumn, a cool breeze in summer, snow in winter. If your mind isn't clouded by unnecessary things, this is the best season of your life.

WU-MEN

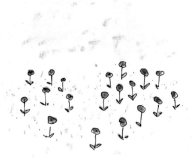

It was a lovely day of blue skies and gentle breezes. Bees buzzed, birds tootled, and squirrels bustled to and fro getting their suntan in the bright sunshine. In a word all nature smiled.

P. G. WODEHOUSE
(1881 – 1975)

A good laugh is sunshine in a house.

WILLIAM MAKEPEACE THACKERAY
(1811 – 1863)

Today a new sun rises for me;
everything lives,
everything is animated,
everything seems to speak
to me of my passion,
everything invites me
to cherish it...

NINON DE L'ENCLOS (1620 – 1705)

Happiness is a lot of things.
It's snow, it's sun – it's a thing
which every day brings.
Happiness is all the world,
the beautiful things around.

EMMA SMITH, AGE 7

Of all happinesses,
the most charming is that of
a firm and gentle friendship.
It sweetens all our cares,
dispels our sorrows, and
counsels us in all extremities.

SENECA THE YOUNGER
(4 B.C. – A.D. 65)

Look at the sky. Look at the river. Look at the trees. Feel, touch, smell. It all belongs to you. You are part of this wonderful creation.

STUART & LINDA MACFARLANE

Learn to greet your friends with a smile;
they carry too many frowns in their own hearts
to be bothered with yours.

MARY ALLETTE AYER

The secret of happiness is to count your blessings while others are adding up their troubles.

WILLIAM PENN (1644 – 1718)

There is so much in the world
for us all if we only
have the eyes to see it,
and the heart to love it,
and the hand to gather
it to ourselves…

LUCY MAUD MONTGOMERY
(1874 – 1942)

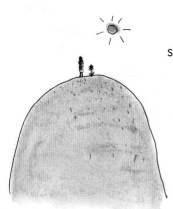

We all experience "soul moments" in life — when we see a magnificent sunrise, hear the call of a loon, see the wrinkles in our mother's hand, or smell the sweetness of a baby. During these moments, our body, as well as our brain, resonates as we experience the glory of being a human being.

MARION WOODMAN, B.1928

May you be able to say
"That was a lovely day."

PAM BROWN

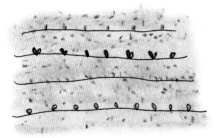

Look.
A line of delicate green
stretched across the earth.
The lettuces have taken.
A little triumph.
A little joy.

PAM BROWN

A single smile…
Could travel round the earth.

BILL CULLEN, B.1942

You can have anything you want
if you want it desperately enough.
You must want it with an exuberance
that erupts through the skin and joins
the energy that created the world.

SHEILA GRAHAM

February 16

✳ ✳ ✳ ✳ ✳ ✳ ✳ ✳ ✳ ✳ ✳ ✳ ✳ ✳ ✳ ✳ ✳

Happiness is a thing of care and consideration, it's everywhere. The birds and the bees show happiness to the trees. The sea and the water show care to the creatures in it. Happiness dominates disaster.

J. QUINNEY

✳ ✳ ✳ ✳ ✳ ✳ ✳ ✳ ✳ ✳ ✳ ✳ ✳ ✳ ✳ ✳ ✳

smile medicine

A smile brightens up
a dreary morning.

STUART & LINDA MACFARLANE

Happiness is a butterfly
which, when pursued,
is always just beyond your grasp,
but which, if you sit down quietly,
may alight upon you.

NATHANIEL HAWTHORNE (1804 – 1864)

People miss their
share of happiness,
not because they never
found it, but because
they didn't stop
to enjoy it.

WILLIAM FEATHER
(1908 – 1976)

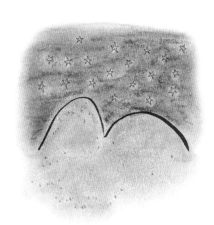

The best way to cheer yourself up
is to try to cheer somebody else up.

MARK TWAIN (1835 – 1910)

May all your kindnesses
be remembered
and all your faults forgiven.

PAM BROWN

The supreme
happiness of life
is the conviction that
we are loved.

VICTOR HUGO
(1802 – 1885)

I was set free! I dissolved in the sea, because white sails and flying spray, became beauty and rhythm, became moonlight and the ship and the high dim-starred sky! I belonged, without past or future, within peace and unity and a wild joy, within something greater than my own life, or the life of Man, to Life itself!

EUGENE O'NEILL (1888 – 1953)

The natural world is positively bursting
with everyday delights: the first crisp days
of autumn; the sight of sun sparkling
on a dewy spider's web;
picking blackberries; a woodpecker
tapping away in your garden.
All these are guaranteed
to make your spirits sing.

MAEVE HARAN

No objects of value…
are worth risking the priceless
experience of waking up
one more day.

JACK SMITH

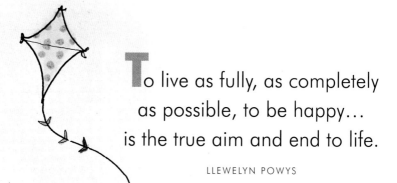

To live as fully, as completely
as possible, to be happy…
is the true aim and end to life.

LLEWELYN POWYS

May you have warm words
on a cold evening,
a full moon on a dark night,
and a smooth road
all the way to your door.

IRISH TOAST

Happiness is a gift made with love and infinite care.

PAM BROWN

The world is so full of wonderful things I think we should all be as happy as kings.

ROBERT LOUIS STEVENSON (1850 – 1894)

You were made for
enjoyment, and the world was
filled with things
which you will enjoy.

JOHN RUSKIN (1819 – 1900)

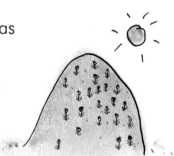

To walk in sunlight along a lonely beach. To sprawl in meadow grass. To swim in the transparency of water. To come home to those you love. That's happiness.

PAM BROWN

Simplicity is the keynote of happiness, and when this fundamental fact is grasped, a great deal of what seems to us essential because we are used to it can be eliminated, and with it much human unhappiness.

FRANK S. SMYTHE (1900 – 1949)

With all its sham,
drudgery and broken
dreams, it is still a
beautiful world.
Be cheerful.
Strive to be happy.

MAX EHRMANN (1872 – 1945)

May you live each second with joy.
May you live each minute with hope.
May you live each hour with patience.
May you live each day with wonder.
And may your year be filled with
peace and love.

STUART & LINDA MACFARLANE

What's happiness?
A thousand things.
And most of them so ordinary
you scarcely notice them.
A cat purring on your knee.
A sudden burst of sunlight
on a winter's day. A plant you
had forgotten flowering.
A thrush. A smile.

PAM BROWN

My friend:
It's the song ye sing,
and the smiles ye wear,
That's a makin' the
sun shine everywhere.

JAMES WHITCOMB RILEY
(1849 – 1916)

May you always know
the happiness of friends.

PAMELA DUGDALE

A blackbird, a mistle thrush and a robin are singing. Mists lie over the fields and the sky is tender blue. At rest in bed in the bare little room, pervaded by light and peace and the sweet airs of morning, there is happiness.

CLARE CAMERON (1896 – 1983)

Let happiness surprise you, like a seashell hidden in the sand...

SUSAN SQUELLATI FLORENCE

February 28/29

May you, today and always,
share the wonder of the world.

May you always choose the path
that leads to the greatest happiness.

PAM BROWN

I arise in the morning torn between a desire to improve the world and a desire to enjoy the world. This makes it hard to plan the day!

E. B. WHITE (1899 – 1985)

The warmth of the sun
on one's hands.
The touch of the wind
on one's cheek.
The sound of a stream.
The scent of the sea.
All happy things.

PAMELA DUGDALE

Love, friendship and generosity – the only ingredients needed for a happy life.

STUART & LINDA MACFARLANE

Stars over snow,
And in the west a planet
Swinging below a star —
Look for a lovely thing
and you will find it,
It is not far —
It never will be far.

SARA TEASDALE (1884 – 1933)

Look to this day! Look to this day! For it is life,
the very life of life. In its brief course lie all the varieties
and realities of your existence: the bliss of growth,
the glory of action, the splendour of beauty.

SANSKRIT

Everybody has their ups and downs so I decided to have mine between good and great.

DAVID HOOGTERP

The rain has lashed the lake, the wind
tumbled the trees. But now it's past.
And all shines, scintillates,
glitters in sudden sunlight.
The world's washed clean.
All dust and drabness gone.
Step out into the bright new day.

PAM BROWN

The only joy in the world is to begin.

CESARE PAVESE (1908 – 1950)

If you're open and smiling,
everybody else picks up on that.

AINSLEY HARRIOTT

The place to be happy is here.
The time to be happy is now.
The way to be happy is to help
make others so.

ROBERT GREEN INGERSOLL
(1833 – 1899)

Never lose an opportunity
of seeing anything that is
beautiful... Welcome beauty
in every fair face, in every
fair sky, in every flower...

RALPH WALDO EMERSON
(1803 – 1882)

My secret joy is found late
at night when a million stars
are reflected in the still surface
of the lake. I paddle out, slip
down to lie on my back in the
bottom of the canoe, and drift
on the water in the silence...
my heart breaking with the
joy of being alive
on this beautiful planet.

ORIAH MOUNTAIN DREAMER

One lonely person.
One other
Lonely person.
One shy smile,
One friendly grin.
Two happy people.

HELEN THOMSON

Let us go singing as far as we go:
the road will be less tedious.

VIRGIL (70 B.C. – 19 B.C.)

Find expression for
a joy, and you will
intensify its ecstasy.

OSCAR WILDE (1854 – 1900)

Happiness is
a great contentment.

PAM BROWN

Gather into yourself like a bee
the hours that fall open
under the bright shaft of the sun
ripening in heat, store them
and make of them
honey days.

NUALA NI DHOMHNAILL, B.1952

The weary miles pass swiftly,
taken in a joyous stride.
And all the world seems
brighter, when a friend
walks by our side.

AUTHOR UNKNOWN

Happiness is both the beginning and end of all the goals you have in your life. And most important, it's the most wonderful feeling in the world.

BILLY MILLS (DAKOTA) WITH NICHOLAS SPARKS

Happiness may
surprise you in simple
moments of being there...
to notice the miracle of
a single morning glory
open to the day.

SUSAN
SQUELLATI FLORENCE

May you have
the happiness of
going on a trip
you never planned
or wanted –
and loving
every moment!

PAM BROWN

To be content
with what we possess
is the greatest
and most secure
of riches.

MARCUS TULLIUS CICERO
(106 B.C. – 43 B.C.)

A small house will hold as much
happiness as a big one.

AUTHOR UNKNOWN

May you drift into sleep saying
"That was a happy day."

PAM BROWN

Stretch out your hand
and take the world's wide
gift of joy and beauty.

CORINNE ROOSEVELT ROBINSON
(1861 – 1933)

The first thing to be done
is laughter, because that sets the
trend for the whole day.

OSHO (1931 – 1990)

Flowers always make people better,
happier, and more helpful; they are sunshine,
food and medicine to the soul.

LUTHER BURBANK (1849 – 1926)

Whenever I've got time
to go somewhere on my bike
I feel happy.
I am free to go wherever
I want. Nobody fussing
around me.
I'm free as a bird.
You can't be happy if
you're not free.

KEVIN WILLIAMS, AGE 9

May you find happiness
everywhere you turn.
In love and friendship
In Music. Theatre. Art.
In mountains, oceans, deserts.
In woods and rivers.
In taste and scent and sound.

CHARLOTTE GRAY

...cheerfulness keeps up a kind of daylight in the mind,
and fills it with a steady and perpetual serenity.

JOSEPH ADDISON (1672 – 1719)

One discovers
one is happy
as suddenly,
as sweetly,
as if one found
one's arms
filled with flowers.

PAM BROWN

To know the reach of one's
abilities, to strive and to achieve
that reach, this is happiness.

PEARL S. BUCK (1892 – 1973)

You have to be willing
to get happy about nothing.

ANDY WARHOL

Happiness is the sun
in the sky,
galloping on the beach,
water splashing,
feeling free.

MEGHAN SIMMONS, AGE 11

Yesterday is but a dream. And tomorrow
is only a vision, but today, well-lived,
makes every yesterday a dream of happiness,
and every tomorrow a vision of hope.
Look well, therefore, to this day.

SANSKRIT

When is it right
to be happy?
Right here
– right now!

STUART & LINDA MACFARLANE

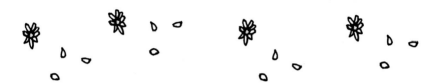

I'm in a wonderful position:
I'm unknown,
I'm underrated, and there's
nowhere to go but up.

PIERRE S. DU PONT IV

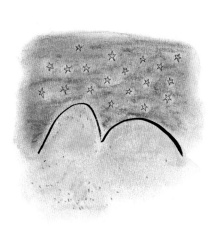

Happiness will allow
you to feel hope in the
darkest of situations and
peace in a world of turmoil.
Happiness will allow your
dreams to come true!
It's the most beautiful
feeling in the world, and it
never has to leave your life!

BILLY MILLS (DAKOTA)
WITH NICHOLAS SPARKS

To find the air and the water exhilarating; to be refreshed by a morning walk or an evening saunter; to find a quest of wild berries more satisfying than a gift of tropical fruit; to be thrilled by the stars at night; to be elated over a bird's nest, or over a wild flower in spring – these are some of the rewards of the simple life.

JOHN BURROUGHS (1837 – 1921)

How simple and frugal
a thing is happiness…
All that is required to feel
that here and now is
happiness is a simple,
frugal heart.

NIKOS KAZANTZAKIS
(1883 – 1957)

Paradise is where I am.

VOLTAIRE (1694 – 1778)

For lo, the winter is past...
Flowers appear on the earth.
The time of the singing birds is
here. The song of the dove
is heard in the land.

SONG OF SOLOMON

May you know
shining days – days
that will brighten
all the dull ones
that lie between.

PAM BROWN

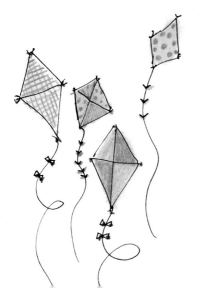

May your life have
diamond days.

PAM BROWN

The beauty of a smile, a smile of love and compassion – that is never lost.

HELEN THOMSON

I have found such joy in things that fill
My quiet days – a curtain's blowing grace,
A growing plant upon a window sill,
A rose fresh-cut and placed within a vase,
A table cleared, a lamp beside a chair,
And books I long have loved beside me there.

GRACE NOLL CROWELL (1877 – 1969)

Thank God every morning
when you get up that you have something
to do that day which must be done,
whether you like it or not.

CHARLES KINGSLEY (1819 – 1875)

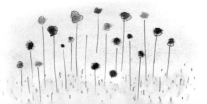

Earth and the great
weather move me...
have carried me away...
and move my inward
parts with joy.

UVAVNUK

Happy are the painters,
for they shall not be lonely.
Light and colour, peace
and hope, shall keep them
to the end of the day.

SIR WINSTON CHURCHILL
(1874 – 1965)

Life is not made up of great sacrifices
and duties, but of little things; in which
smiles and kindness given habitually are
what win and preserve the heart.

SIR HUMPHREY DAVY (1778 – 1829)

If you're seeking freedom
seek it on the mountains,
God's sunlight on
your shoulders,
the wind in your hair.

J. DONALD WALTERS

Today happiness knocks...
And every day.

PAM BROWN

May you know contentment, delight, and your fair share of absolute joy.

PAM BROWN

...an act of goodness is in itself an act of happiness.
It is the flower of a long inner life of joy and contentment;
it tells of peaceful hours and days on the sunniest heights
of our soul.

COUNT MAURICE MAETERLINCK (1862 – 1949)

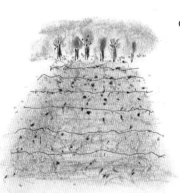

We spend a day doing most
ordinary things, but among people
that we love, in the clear sunlight
of the first of spring,
busy and content.
And go to bed at last and smile –
"That was a lovely day."
And sleep wrapped
in happiness.

PAMELA DUGDALE

March 28

Everyday happiness means getting up in the morning, and you can't wait to finish your breakfast. You can't wait to do your exercises. You can't wait to put on your clothes. You can't wait to get out – and you can't wait to come home, because the soup is hot.

GEORGE BURNS (1896 – 1996)

Having only coarse food
to eat, plain water to drink,
and a bent arm for a pillow, one
can still find happiness therein.

CONFUCIUS (551 B.C. – 479 B.C.)

I wish the hills
were full of music
And everybody sang.
Happy hours we'd spend
In the sun filled days.

MORWENNA POND, AGE 8

When we have a happy heart,
we move forward. We dive
deep within. We fly.

SRI CHINMOY (1931 – 2007)

Each day is a gift.
Open it.
Celebrate.
Enjoy it.

STUART & LINDA MACFARLANE

Talk about the joys of the unexpected, can they compare with the joys of the expected, of finding everything delightfully and completely what you knew it was going to be?

ELIZABETH BIBESCO
(1897 – 1945)

The best and sweetest things in life are things you cannot buy: the music of the birds at dawn, the rainbow in the sky. The dazzling magic of the stars, the miracle of light.

PATIENCE STRONG
(1907 – 1990)

October 4

The things that make me happy are flowers
diamonds and butterflies and ladybirds all
things that are coloured and clowns make
me laugh and the sun and summer
and the snow makes me happy and toys
makes me and sweets and the hedgehogs
are nice although they are prickly.

ELIZABETH WRIGHT

I hope you find joy
in the great things
of life – but also
in the little things.
A flower,
a song, a butterfly
on your hand.

ELLEN LEVINE

A smile creates sunshine in the home... fosters goodwill in business... and is the best antidote for trouble.

AUTHOR UNKNOWN

The weather forecast says "Rain! Rain! Rain!" but your heart says "Sun! Sun! Sun!"

STUART & LINDA MACFARLANE

Happiness is a journey
where nothing goes wrong.
The connection is simple.
And someone is waiting
for you. Smiling.

PAM BROWN

When you finally allow yourself to trust joy and embrace it, you will find you dance with everything.

EMMANUEL

The best way to secure
future happiness
is to be as happy as is
rightfully possible today.

CHARLES W. ELIOT
(1834 – 1926)

One of the healthiest
ways to gamble
is with a spade
and a package
of garden seeds.

DAN BENNETT

May all your
dreams be happy.
May all your
sleep be sound.

PAM BROWN

It is by believing, hoping, loving
and doing that people find joy and peace.

JOHN LANCASTER SPALDING (c.1609 – 1670)

My advice is:
Go outside, to the fields,
enjoy nature
and the sunshine,
go out and try to
recapture happiness...

ANNE FRANK
(1929 – 1945)

Sunshine is delicious,
rain is refreshing, wind braces
us up, snow is exhilarating;
there is really no such thing
as bad weather, only different
kinds of good weather.

JOHN RUSKIN (1819 – 1900)

Increase your happy times, letting yourself go; follow your desire and best advantage. And "do your thing" while you are still on this earth, according to the command of your heart.

"SONG OF ARTUF"
AFRICAN PROVERB

Each day
provides its
own gifts.

MARTIAL (c.40 – c.104)

Day and night
I shall swim in the
sweetness-hope-river.

SRI CHINMOY
(1931 – 2007)

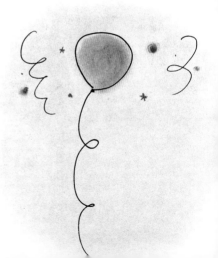

Happiness is a warm feeling in your tummy.

TRACEY DOWSON, AGE 8

These are the things I prize
and hold of deepest worth:
Light of the sapphire skies,
peace of the silent hills,
shelter of the forests...
But best of all, along the way,
friendship and mirth.

HENRY VAN DYKE (1852 – 1933)

Don't hurry, don't worry.
You're only here for a short visit. So be sure
to stop and smell the flowers.

WALTER HAGEN (1892 – 1969)

All problems fade out
in proportion as you develop
this ability to be quiet, to
behold and to witness divine
harmony unfold.

JOEL S. GOLDSMITH

The blue of heaven
is larger than the cloud.

ELIZABETH BARRETT
BROWNING (1806 – 1861)

The world is really
a wonderful place. Each day,
acts of kindness outnumber
the atrocities by an unimaginable
factor. Seek out and focus on the
positive and try your very best not
to be affected by anything negative.

STUART & LINDA MACFARLANE

To make me happy I would like
to make other people happy. I want to
be nice and to help people.
I want to enjoy every minute of my life
by helping all the people in the world
when they are poorly.

LISA STANLEY, AGE 7

Joy seems to me a stop beyond happiness – happiness is
a sort of atmosphere you can live in sometimes when you are lucky.
Joy is a light that fills you with the hope and faith and love.

ADELA ROGERS ST. JOHN

May your life always be full of new discoveries.

PAM BROWN

Laughter can be more
satisfying than honour;
more precious than money;
more heart-cleansing
than prayer.

HARRIET ROCHLIN

I still find each day too
short for all the thoughts
I want to think, all the walks
I want to take, all the books
I want to read,
and all the friends
I want to see.

JOHN BURROUGHS (1837 – 1921)

I feel glad as the ponies do when the fresh green grass starts in the beginning of the year.

TEN BEARS, YAMPARETHKA
COMANCHE CHIEF

...the little hills rejoice
on every side. The pastures
are clothed with flocks;
the valleys also are covered
over with corn; they shout
for joy, they also sing.

PSALMS 65:12-13

With mirth and laughter
let old wrinkles come.

WILLIAM SHAKESPEARE (1564 – 1616)

Three grand essentials to happiness in this life
are something to do,
something to love, and something to hope for.

JOSEPH ADDISON (1672 – 1719)

I've learned that for a happy day, look for something bright and beautiful in nature. Listen for a beautiful sound, speak a kind word to some person, and do something nice for someone without their knowledge.

AUTHOR UNKNOWN

All shall be well,
and all shall be well and all
manner of things shall be well.

JULIAN OF NORWICH
(c.1342 – 1416)

Still there is joy that
will not cease,
Calm hovering o'er
the face of things,
That sweet tranquillity
and peace
That morning ever brings.

JOHN CLARE
(1793 – 1864)

Good things
happen to millions
of people every day.
Because so many have
shared the same things does
not make the joy less –
it makes it more.

ROSIE SWALE POPE

We know nothing of tomorrow;
our business is to be good
and happy today.

SYDNEY SMITH (1771 – 1845)

The hillside's dew-pearled;
The lark's on the wing;
The snail's on the thorn;
God's in his heaven,
All's right with the world!

ROBERT BROWNING
(1812 – 1889)

I roll out of my couch
every morning with the most
agreeable expectations.

H. L. MENCKEN
(1880 – 1956)

My advice to you
is not to inquire why or
whither, but just enjoy
your ice cream while
it's on your plate
– that's my philosophy.

THORNTON WILDER
(1897 – 1976)

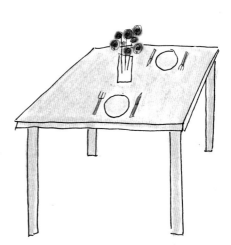

You're only fully alive
when you're happy.
Go For It!

STUART & LINDA MACFARLANE

Take time to be friendly –
It is the road to happiness.
Take time to love and to be loved –
It is the privilege of the gods.
Take time to look around –
It is too short a day to be selfish.
Take time to laugh –
It is the music of the soul.

FROM AN OLD ENGLISH SAMPLER

Acquire the habit of expecting success,
of believing in happiness. Nothing succeeds like
success; nothing makes happiness like happiness.

LILIAN WHITING

Each and every new
day brings a fresh start,
a new beginning, a new
world full of opportunities
and possibilities.
It's a wonderful world.

STUART & LINDA MACFARLANE

September 13

When the clouds are floating by.
And the day goes by and by.
We should all be smiling.
Not stuck in a office filing.

M. GURR, AGE 10

It's a funny thing about happiness...
it just sort of sneaks up on you.
Some days I feel happy because of the way
the light strikes things.
Or for some beautifully immature reason
like finding myself running to the kitchen
to make some toast.

JONI MITCHELL, B.1943

September 12

Happiness is built
on simple foundations –
The love of beauty,
A sense of humour,
The gift of good friends.

FROM "THE FRIENDSHIP BOOK
OF FRANCIS GAY"

The best wake-up call
I know is to have my son smile
at me in the morning.

SEAN PERTWEE

May you not miss
the happiness in little things
while waiting for
the great delights.

PAM BROWN

May you turn
the corner
of an uneventful day
and find wonder.

PAM BROWN

Every word and every being come knocking at your door, bringing you their mystery. If you are open to them, they will flood you with their riches.

IRÉNÉE GUILANE DIOH, B.1948

The importance of a happy life
can't be exaggerated.
Think of each and every day as priceless.
If you take a series of those days
and combine them, it becomes a year.
Add the years together, and it becomes
a lifetime – a lifetime of love, happiness,
honor, hopes, and dreams.

BILLY MILLS (DAKOTA) WITH NICHOLAS SPARKS

Live in each season as it passes, breathe the air, drink the drink, taste the fruit, and resign yourself to the influences of each.

HENRY DAVID THOREAU (1817 – 1862)

Beauty breaks out
everywhere –
in the smile on an aged
face and on the timeless
tracts of
the countryside.

FROM "GRACE" MAGAZINE

Real happiness comes from inside. Nobody can give it to you.
I think I'm happiest when I'm playing with my goddaughter,
happiest when I'm riding horses, when I'm with friends,
when I'm cooking dinner, when I'm in a darkened audience
watching a performer I admire.

SHARON STONE, B.1958

Every day
is a good day.

YUN MEN (c. 863 – 949)

Daring enthusiasm and abiding
cheerfulness can accomplish everything
on earth without fail.

SRI CHINMOY (1931 – 2007)

Suddenly,
somewhere, some day —
we find
that we are happy.

AMY POTTER

Optimists
may be wrong
just as often as
pessimists —
but they have
more fun.

FROM
"THE FRIENDSHIP BOOK
OF FRANCIS GAY"

How beautiful a day can be
when kindness touches it!

GEORGE ELLISTON

A coin down
the side of the sofa.
A woodpecker in the garden.
A cup of coffee with a friend.
May you find happiness
every single day.

PAMELA DUGDALE

One must never look
for happiness:
one meets it by the way...

ISABELLE EBERHARDT
(1877 – 1904)

To be aged to perfection
and happy. To dance. To run.
To walk for miles along the shore.
To sing. Gather it up.
Store it like honey to shine
with a golden light, to bring
a sweetness to your whole life.

CHARLOTTE GRAY

May every day bring
some new happiness.

PAMELA DUGDALE

The more you praise
and celebrate your life,
the more there is in life
to celebrate.

OPRAH WINFREY, B.1954

You are not fully dressed
until you put a smile on.

EVAN ESAR (1899 – 1995)

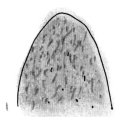

May you never lose
your joy in little pleasures.
Sunlight after rain.
Tea with a friend.
Deep and gentle sleep.

PAM BROWN

Let happiness be yours today
as you find what brings you beauty…
the fresh flowers on your table,
the fragile seashell on your desk.

SUSAN SQUELLATI FLORENCE

Is it so small a thing
To have enjoy'd the sun,
To have lived light in the spring,
To have loved, to have thought,
to have done…

MATTHEW ARNOLD (1822 – 1888)

One small surprise…
A letter. A lost thing found.
Kindness from a stranger.
A skein of geese strewn
across the sky.
Celandines in the ditch.
A perfect batch of scones.
A ring around the moon.

AMY POTTER

Sun shining through
the curtains as you wake.
A soft rain falling.
Leaf buds opening to spring.
A cuckoo calling.
Here's happiness.

PAM BROWN

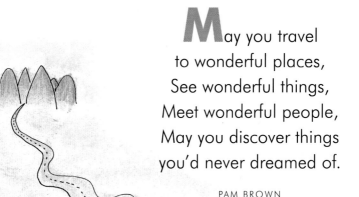

May you travel
to wonderful places,
See wonderful things,
Meet wonderful people,
May you discover things
you'd never dreamed of.

PAM BROWN

You have not lived a perfect day,
even though you have earned your money,
unless you have done something for someone
who will never be able to repay you.

RUTH SMELTZER

The possibilities of happiness are all around us,
if we would only open our eyes and give thanks.

JONATHAN SACKS

Existence is a strange bargain.
Life owes us little; we owe it
everything. The only true happiness
comes from squandering ourselves
for a purpose.

WILLIAM COWPER
(1731 – 1800)

May you find happiness
in both the central and the
smallest, quietest, gentle,
little things.

JENNY DE VRIES

Normal day, let me
be aware of the treasure you are.
Let me learn from you, love you,
bless you before you depart.
Let me not pass you by in quest
of some rare and perfect tomorrow.
Let me hold you while
I may, for it may not always be so.

MARY JEAN IRION

The best day is... today!

AUTHOR UNKNOWN

There is a wonderful, mystical law of nature that the three things we crave most in life – happiness, freedom, and peace of mind – are always attained by giving them to someone else.

PEYTON CONWAY MARCH
(1864 – 1955)

The one that lives in hope dances without music.

GEORGE HERBERT (1593 – 1633)

If you feel no enthusiasm or inspiration
on a particular day, try to remember a joyful experience
from your past. The joy you got from your
previous achievements will carry you through.

SRI CHINMOY (1931 – 2007)

This is no dress rehearsal for life, this is a live performance — so stop worrying and enjoy the show.

STUART & LINDA
MACFARLANE

We have no right
to happiness. It is an
astounding gift.

PAM BROWN

Write it on your heart
that every day is the
best day of the year.

RALPH WALDO EMERSON
(1803 – 1882)

Frame your mind to mirth
and merriment,
which bars
a thousand harms and
lengthens life.

WILLIAM SHAKESPEARE
(1564 – 1616)

Happiness is a hug
after loneliness.
Is sunlight after storm.
Spring after winter's ravages.
The lights of home.

CHARLOTTE GRAY

Sometimes days only take a burst of sunshine, a clump of daffodils, a song to flood the heart with happiness.

PAM BROWN

We search for happiness
everywhere, but we are like
Tolstoy's fabled beggar who spent
his life sitting on a pot of gold,
begging for pennies from every
passerby, unaware that his fortune
was right under him the whole
time. Your treasure – your
perfection – is within you already.

ELIZABETH GILBERT, B.1969

Beauty is the flowers opening their faces. Beauty is the larks gliding over dark blue clouds. Beauty is the snowflakes drifting down on my head. Beauty is the moonlight creeping up behind huge mountains. Beauty is for plants growing higher, higher, and higher.

MANDY GIBSON, AGE 10

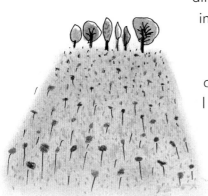

I have smelt
all the aromas there are
in the fragrant kitchen
they call Earth;
and what we
can enjoy in this life,
I surely have enjoyed
just like a lord!

HEINRICH HEINE
(1797 – 1856)

You have your brush, you have your colours,
you paint paradise, then in you go.

NIKOS KAZANTZAKIS (1883 – 1957)

All our dreams can
come true – if we have the courage
to pursue them.

WALT DISNEY
(1901 – 1966)

I wish you friends,
kind friends who care for you
when you are low, who can
teach you to laugh again.

HELEN EXLEY

Never has
the earth
been so lovely
nor the sun
so bright,
as today...

NIKINAPI

The aim of life is to live, and to live means to be aware, joyously, drunkenly, serenely, divinely aware.

HENRY MILLER (1891 – 1980)

The sun shines.
The rain falls.
The grass grows –
The world is doing
just what it should.

STUART &
LINDA MACFARLANE

May the longtime sun shine
upon you, all love surround you,
and the sweet light within you
guide you on your way.

SNATAM KAUR

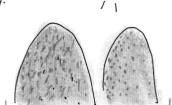

Happiness is
a friend arriving unexpectedly
on an empty day.

PAM BROWN

A bird. A flower. A cloud,
a gleam of sun.
A smile. A touch. A word.
Happiness comes in a
thousand guises.

PAM BROWN

Happiness is meant for everyone
but is elusive as a butterfly.
Happiness is beautiful, as a flower.
It cannot be expressed in any rhyme.
It may only last a fraction of an hour.
But it stays inside the heart
beyond all time.

E. WRIGHT

I expand and live
in the warm day like
corn and melons.

RALPH WALDO EMERSON
(1803 – 1882)

To make a people happy,
add not to their riches,
but take away their desires.

EPICURUS (341 B.C. – 270 B.C.)

How to be happy: Keep your heart free from hate, your mind from worry, live simply, expect little, give much, sing often, pray always, forget self, think of others and their feelings, fill your heart with love, scatter sunshine. These are tried links in the golden chain of contentment.

NORMAN VINCENT PEALE
(1898 – 1993)

There are times when the heart and mind are overwhelmed by silence. Times when the roaring world retreats and leaves us to discover peace. So brief a respite. Cherish the moment.

PAM BROWN

My heart leaps up when I behold
A rainbow in the sky:
So was it when my life began;
So it is now I am a man:
So be it when I shall grow old,
Or let me die!

WILLIAM WORDSWORTH
(1770 – 1850)

The world would be a much better place
if everyone smiled more. So smile, be cheerful.

MOTHER TERESA (1910 – 1997)

Earth's crammed
with heaven.

ELIZABETH BARRETT BROWNING
(1806 – 1861)

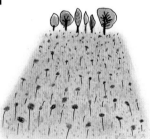

The true harvest of my daily life is somewhat as intangible and indescribable as the tints of morning or evening. It is a little stardust caught, a segment of the rainbow which I have clutched.

HENRY DAVID THOREAU
(1817 – 1862)

May this day be
a day to remember.

PAM BROWN

The most complete happiness
is to work at something you love.
And to do it to the best
of your ability.

PAM BROWN

...the secret of happiness
is realising that we have it now.

FROM "THE FRIENDSHIP BOOK OF FRANCIS GAY"

There are only
two ways to live your life.
One is as though
nothing is a miracle.
The other is as though
everything is a miracle.

ALBERT EINSTEIN (1879 – 1955)

The day began with dismal doubt
A stubborn thing to put to rout;
But all my worries flew away
When someone smiled at me today.

AUTHOR UNKNOWN

Happiness is yours in all nature…
in fields of wildflowers and silent deep
forests, in the mystical mountains,
and the song of a distant bird.

SUSAN SQUELLATI FLORENCE

...this was the simple happiness of complete harmony with her surroundings, the happiness that asks for nothing, that just accepts, just breathes, just is.

COUNTESS VON ARNIM
(1866 – 1941)

To be interested
in the changing seasons
is a happier state of mind
than to be hopelessly
in love with spring.

GEORGE SANTAYANA
(1863 – 1952)

Keep a green tree
in our heart and perhaps
a singing bird will come.

CHINESE PROVERB

Keep your face to the
sunshine and you cannot
see the shadow.

HELEN KELLER (1880 – 1968)

Whether seventy or sixteen, there is in every being's heart a love of wonder; the sweet amazement at the stars and starlike things and thoughts; the undaunted challenge of events, the unfailing childlike appetite for what comes next, and the joy in the game of life.

SAMUEL ULLMAN

Life begins
every morning when
you wake up.

GEORGE BURNS
(1896 – 1996)

...the most beautiful smiles
in the world are the ones that struggle
through the tears.

AUTHOR UNKNOWN

I like living. I have sometimes been wildly, despairingly, acutely miserable, racked with sorrow, but through it all I still know quite certainly that just to be alive is a grand thing.

AGATHA CHRISTIE (1890 – 1976)

Joy is the realization
of oneness of our soul,
the oneness of our soul
with the world and of
the world soul...

RABINDRANATH TAGORE
(1861 – 1941)

Suddenly the heart lifts with joy
– finding itself part of all that is.
Sunlight and cloud,
trees, rivers, wild geese flying.
A moment's glory.

CHARLOTTE GRAY

To experience happiness is to experience freedom. No matter what may happen in life, nothing will be able to touch true happiness.

THE MONKS OF NEW SKETE

Travel lightly.
Happiness
is inclined
to get lost
in the luggage.

PAM BROWN

It's the scent of the roses that fills the air,
and the whispering wind blowing through my hair.
It's the sparkling dewdrops on the ground,
and the gurgling stream that makes hardly a sound.
It's the feel of the snowflakes that melt on my tongue.
And the night owl calling to her young.

ELIZABETH ANNE DE GREY

True joy is serene.

SENECA THE YOUNGER (4 B.C. – A.D. 65)

August 2

Take time out to think about
an enjoyable occasion from your
childhood – a birthday party or
a trip to the zoo or making
sandcastles on the beach.
For a few moments let yourself
be that child again.

STUART & LINDA MACFARLANE

Just Stop!
Right Now!
Don't do anything.
Don't think anything
just BE!
WOW! Isn't life FANTASTIC!

STUART & LINDA MACFARLANE

Yesterday is a cancelled cheque;
tomorrow is a promissory note;
today is the only cash you have
— so spend it wisely.

KAY LYONS

Works of love
are always works of joy.
We don't need to look
for happiness: if we have love
for others we'll be given it.

MOTHER TERESA (1910 – 1997)

Sally has a smile
I would accept as my last
view of earth.

WALLACE STEGNER (1909 – 1993)

Hope is something sweet, divine, and encouraging.

SRI CHINMOY (1931 – 2007)

May all your beginnings
be strong and true — whether
a plant, a tree, an idea,
A song, a book, a cabinet,
an engine. A family...

CHARLOTTE GRAY

A smile is an investment,
an inner happy glow.
a mood-lifter,
a cheer-giver.

KATY CLARKE

It's good for your spirit,
remember that, to give a smile.

MOLLY DARCY (1892 – 1992)

The only tragedy
in life is that there's
so much fun to be had
that there could never
be enough time
to cram it all in.

STUART & LINDA MACFARLANE

And remember this: every time we laugh,
we take a kink out of the chain of life.

JOSH BILLINGS (1818 – 1885)

Happiness is riding
Happiness is free
Happiness is jumping
So it must be me!

ANDREW TROWBRIDGE, AGE 7

DANCE, my heart;
Oh, dance today with joy!

KABIR (1380 – 1420)

The happiest person is the one
who thinks the happiest thoughts.

NORMAN VINCENT PEALE (1898 – 1993)

There is one thing which gives radiance to everything. It is the idea of something around the corner.

G. K. CHESTERTON
(1874 – 1936)

I have found such joy in simple things:
A plain, clean room, a nut-brown loaf of bread,
A cup of milk, a kettle as it sings,
The shelter of a roof above my head,
And in a leaf-laced square along the floor,
Where yellow sunlight glimmers through a door.

GRACE NOLL CROWELL (1877 – 1969)

True happiness comes from
the joy of deeds well done,
the zest of creating things new.

ANTOINE DE SAINT-EXUPERY
(1900 – 1944)

Happiness is found
in the very littlest things.

CHARLOTTE GRAY

Live all you can;
it's a mistake not to.
It doesn't so much
matter what you do in
particular so long as
you have your life.

HENRY JAMES (1843 – 1916)

There are persons so radiant,
so genial, so kind,
so pleasure-bearing,
that you instinctively feel,
in their presence,
that they do you good,
that their coming into a room
is like bringing a lamp there.

HENRY WARD BEECHER (1813 – 1887)

July 23

Sadness hears
the clock strike every hour,
Happiness forgets
the day of the month.

SENECA THE YOUNGER
(4 B.C. – A.D. 65)

Life – the most wonderful fairground attraction of all
– enjoy the ride.

STUART & LINDA MACFARLANE

...there's the real danger of
overlooking a very important day...
today. For this is the place
and the time for living.
Let us live each day
abundantly and beautifully
while it is here.

ESTHER BALDWIN YORK

The art of being happy lies
in the power of extracting
happiness from common things.

HENRY WARD BEECHER
(1813 – 1887)

Sun, and sky, and breeze, and solitary walks,
and summer holidays, and the greenness of fields…
and society, and the cheerful glass, and candlelight,
and fireside conversations and innocent
vanities and jests.

CHARLES LAMB (1775 – 1834)

Close your eyes. You might try saying… something like this:
"The sun is shining overhead. The sky is blue and sparkling.
Nature is calm and in control of the world –
and I, as nature's child, am in tune with the Universe."

DALE CARNEGIE (1888 – 1955)

Happiness
is cutting through
a fresh crusty loaf.

CLIVE GARLAND, AGE 12

May your days be filled with laughter.
Spluttering laughter, whooping laughter.
The laughter that crowns success,
that springs from joy.

PAM BROWN

People are always happy
for having been happy; so that,
if you make them happy now,
you make them happy twenty years
hence by the memory of it.

SYDNEY SMITH (1771 – 1845)

Sixty seconds in every minute
– 3600 in every hour
– each one a precious diamond
to cherish and enjoy.

STUART & LINDA MACFARLANE

O wonderful, wonderful,
and most wonderful
wonderful, and yet again
wonderful, and after
that out of all whooping!

WILLIAM SHAKESPEARE (1564 – 1616)

One today
is worth two
tomorrows.

BENJAMIN FRANKLIN
(1706 – 1790)

I look up
– and laugh
– and love
– and lift.

HOWARD ARNOLD WALTER

A place in which
we are wanted,
in which there is someone
to whom we matter
more than anything
in the world,
of such a place
are the four walls made.

FROM "GRACE" MAGAZINE

To be completely happy
is rarer than we believe.
Enjoy it to the utmost –
but let it go without regret.

PAM BROWN

The human race has only one really effective weapon and that is laughter. Against the assault of laughter nothing can stand.

MARK TWAIN (1835 – 1910)

To become a happy person,
have a clean soul, eyes
that see romance in the
commonplace, a child's heart,
and spiritual simplicity.

NORMAN VINCENT PEALE (1898 – 1993)

The shimmer of sun
on meadow grass.
The glitter of rain wet leaves.
The surge of a gale among
the trees. The hush of surf
along the shore.
Here's happiness.

PAM BROWN

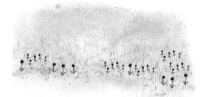

Live your Joy,
Go against the grain.
Don't be made timid by worried
rejection. Let nature's curious
wisdom fill you. Let the world's
mystical heritage guide you.
Paint your canvases,
play your tunes.

SIR THOMAS MORE
(1478 – 1535)

True happiness is...
to enjoy the present,
without anxious
dependence upon
the future.

SENECA THE YOUNGER
(4 B.C. – A.D 65.)

May I a small house
and a large garden have;
And a few friends,
and many books, both true,
both wise, and both
delightful too!

ABRAHAM COWLEY (1618 – 1667)

Keep on looking for
the bright, bright skies;
Keep on hoping that the
sun will rise;
Keep on singing when
the whole world sighs,
And you'll get there
in the morning.

HENRY "HARRY" THACKER BURLEIGH
(1866 – 1949)

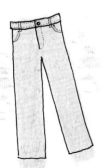

People need joy quite as much as clothing. Some of them need it far more.

MARGARET COLLIER GRAHAM

Oh, the enchantment when, waking from deep sleep, we open up the house to the sounds of the world! How the morning air invigorates, caressing the senses and penetrating our whole being! The tang of it, the welcome it draws from us – they take us by surprise.

IRÉNÉE GUILANE DIOH, B.1948

Happiness is the smell of the air on summer mornings cool and crisp.

LEE WALKER, AGE 8

Go lightly, like a butterfly,
and find what fills you...
what enlivens you...
what you love.

SUSAN SQUELLATI FLORENCE

To fill the hour – that is happiness; to fill the hour, and leave no crevice for a repentance or an approval.

RALPH WALDO EMERSON
(1803 – 1882)

GREETINGS ON THIS DAY!

May it be a day to remember.
And may the coming year bring you new joy,
new friendships, new beginnings.

AMEEN MOHAMMED

Peace is always beautiful.

WALT WHITMAN (1819 – 1892)

There is only one happiness in life,
to love and be loved.

GEORGE SAND (AMANDINE AURORE LUCILE DUPIN)
(1804 – 1876)

A day of doing
nothing special –
but with someone you love.
Happiness need
not be spectacular.

PAM BROWN

Each day has a rarity...
I could put it in a vase
and admire it,
like the first dandelions...

MARGARET LAWRENCE

Be HAPPY
Be Free.

MARTIN BURNETT, AGE 10

It's just the little homely things,
The unobtrusive, friendly things,
The "Won't-you-let-me-help-you"
things... That make the world
seem bright.

AUTHOR UNKNOWN

One of life's great secrets is surely to celebrate the small – the sight of a flower growing between the cracks in a pavement, the look on a young child's face when they're given a birthday present they've waited for long weeks to open. Or something as simple as immersing ourselves in our favourite piece of music.

FROM "THE FRIENDSHIP BOOK OF FRANCIS GAY"

Happiness is lying
in bed on gloomy
misty mornings.

ADRIAN KNIGHT, AGE 10

Happiness happens only in the present moment.
If you are happy now, there is nothing else to accomplish.
Indeed, if you become concerned about whether you
will be happy tomorrow or even five minutes
from now, you will forget to be happy now.

PAUL FERRINI

Long after I have forgotten all
my human loves, I shall still remember
the smell of a gooseberry leaf,
or the feel of wet grass on my bare feet.
In the long run, it is this feeling that
makes life worth living...

GWEN RAVERAT

Laughing stirs up the blood, expands the chest, electrifies the nerves, clears away the cobwebs from the brain, and gives the whole system a cleansing rehabilitation.

AUTHOR UNKNOWN

Happiness is yours today in doing whatever interests you, excites you or challenges you.

SUSAN SQUELLATI FLORENCE

The day is over.
But here in my hands
I hold a glow,
the happiness it brought
to see me through the night.

PAM BROWN

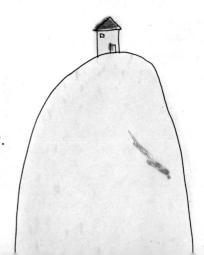